Messages
from the Stream

Alicia Conklin-Wood

WILLOW STREET, PA 2016

Cover and Interior Book Design: Kate Boyer
Cover Photo: Alicia Conklin-Wood

To contact Author:
acwbook@gmail.com

For Online Book Orders:
www.createspace.com/6559142

ISBN 978-0692782743

Printed in the United States of America

Contents

III Autumn

Introduction: Messages from the Stream

The frequent walks I take are an important part of my spiritual life whether I am at home or away. For me, these outings are not only a form of exercise but also a time of reflection and centering within the activities of my daily life. They've come to be an integral part of my spiritual practice-- listening for the messages from God, Christ, Spirit, Love or simply the Sacred Mystery, that come to us when we tune in to the currents that run somewhere just below the surface of our lives.

On the days when I'm walking near my home, I make a habit of stopping at a little stream that runs under a nearby road. It's actually more of a rill, the headwaters of a larger stream. Late summer's dry spells often leave it shallow. Sometimes it hardly seems to flow at all, but then I spot a trickle among a stretch of rocks that emerges to flow smoothly again for a distance. Life can seem like that, too, during a time of spiritual drought. At those times, it can be hard to see the activity of the Holy. It comforts me to sense that, even though I can't see or feel it, a holy spirit is flowing through all of life carrying me to a new place where life will again flow smoothly, for a time.

Other streams and places offer their messages, too, and I've developed a practice of listening for them wherever I may be. When I'm away on retreat, these messages often seem to come during my walks, which often can take an unexpected turn—as in the reflection that follows.

Most of us have had the experience of setting out for one goal, only to discover that we were being led instead in another direction. In the life of the spirit, this so often seems to be the way. So it was for me one early spring day.

I was away on retreat just south of Buffalo NY, and I'd bundled up well against a wind that was fierce and bitterly cold. I remembered that in scriptures, Spirit often comes as wind, and that helped to set my intention for the outing. I decided to open myself to whatever guidance might come to me on this walk. I'd set out meaning to return to a wonderful "sitting" rock that I'd found on an earlier walk. I was also determined to find a waterfall I'd been told about. Through the shelter of the woods and across the meadow I hiked, picking up the path into the woods on the other side.

In the beginning the path seemed mostly easy—that is, until I slipped on a muddy section. Ugh. I gathered myself up and continued downhill beyond the mud. I could see a turn in the path farther down, but it wasn't passable. I struck out cross-country instead, on a parallel route of my own making through a tangle of vines and brambles. As I scrambled through I tried to hang onto one old dead tree for support, but it broke off and fell. I began to ponder how I sometimes try to hang onto the "deadwood" of my past: old beliefs, childhood "tapes," outworn behaviors.

Once I reached the bottom of the hill, I noticed a clearing. Between it and myself flowed a stream. Unable to cross it to reach the clearing, I turned left instead onto a narrow path that looked as if it might take me to Cazenovia Creek. *It can't be far*, I thought, and so I set out for the creek. But first I had to cross a small brook. Just at the point when I most needed help in the crossing, I saw a smooth stone that someone had put in the middle of the stream bed. A stepping stone—what a gift. It led me to reflect on the "stepping stones" in life that have been given to me when I sorely needed them.

Then, a little farther on, I came to yet another brook that was very muddy on both sides. It was April, and the brook ran full with spring runoff. No matter. I'd already begun to feel pretty sure I wasn't going to find either my sitting rock or the waterfall. I also had a growing sense that, through all these little obstacles, I was being led on a journey. I just didn't yet know to what destination. I went ahead and crossed the brook. Just on the other side and up a little knoll I entered a lovely moss-covered grove—beyond which was the edge of Cazenovia Creek.

How did I get to this amazing place? I wondered. *So clear, so clean and inviting.* Here, one of the little brooks I'd already forded opened out and tumbled down over layers of granite and slate, falling to the creek below. The water that flowed there was too smooth and graceful to be called a rapids, though I suppose that's what it was. The stream at one point turned back in on itself, forming a small pool—almost like the pool of Siloam in the Bible, I thought.

Finally aware that this was the place to which I'd been led, I vowed to make a daily pilgrimage there while I was on retreat. For this special place, where the sun shone brightly and the waters flowed clear, was now my place of rest and worship—a gift.

In every season of life, spring, summer, fall, and winter, I've learned how much it matters to pay attention to these "messages from the stream," whether the stream is a literal one of water or the currents of our lives. They offer messages that speak of life, of love, and of the sacredness of all life, and it is their wisdom that inspired this book.

The Many Names for God

As some of my readers will know, the Bible has many names for God. Just try keeping a list as I once did. Each of us also has favorite names that connect us with the Holy One, names like Father, Good Shepherd, Holy, One, Washer woman God (on laundry days), etc. The Quaker tradition often uses light as a metaphor for God, reminding us of the sacred light within us and all things. My seminary Hebrew studies taught me to appreciate some of the feminine names for the Holy of Holies that have gotten lost in all the Biblical translations. One example is in the Book of Deuteronomy when the story is told of how God brought the Israelites out of Egypt "as on Eagles wings". Ornithologists recognize this immediately as a feminine image, but most translations still speak of how "he" brought them out." And so it goes. In recent years I've also discovered and sometimes use the word "Godde", a word that recognizes both the masculine and feminine aspects of the Divine Being. And, recent hymnals contain one of my favorite hymns, *Bring Many Names*. Whatever name is used, the One we worship and serve, and to whom we are drawn ever closer is bigger than any one name or description. What word are you drawn to when trying to name this great Mystery, this Being of Light and Love?

Bibles

Although there are several excellent versions of the Bible, I usually use the New Revised Standard Version (NRSV) and so have used it here for references.

How to use this book

Messages from the Stream is divided into four main sections, one for each season of the year in the northern hemisphere. This helps me put specific sections dealing with Christmas in winter and sweltering hot days in summer. I have begun with Spring, a season of renewed hope, although any season can offer signs of hope. Regardless of the order, I invite you to simply pick it up from time to time and read one or two, or a few, reflections, allowing time to pause and feel how they connect with your life. Perhaps the questions at the end of each piece will be a guide for you, or perhaps you will want to sit quietly with the reading and let a meaning evolve especially for you. These reflections are not meant to be read hurriedly, nor necessarily sequentially. Read, pause, and listen deeply for the message from the Holy One for you.

Acknowledgements

There are so many people who have helped me along the way to this book, encouraging, prodding, inspiring, reading early pieces, it's hard to name everyone. My husband Len and children Beth, David and Michael have all been patient and encouraging for the ten years this book has taken for me to write it. They, along with special people like Gladys Lehman, Gary Meier, Fran Carr, and JoAnn Macdonald have each read some sections, offering helpful advice, listened to my concerns or progress reports over and over again. My spiritual director Nancy Bieber has faithfully held the sacred space for me and gently prodded me from time to time to continue the work. The Tuesday group that meets monthly at our home gave me helpful feedback after reading sections, and recently asked when they could read the whole book!

I could never have brought this book to print without the help of my two editors, Dana Knighton and Kate Boyer. For their patience and enormous help I owe them much gratitude.

I want to thank these and all the unnamed friends who have supported me on this project, my first book. Finally, in this book I speak of the One called Light and Love who comes to us in many ways. Truly I am most grateful for the Spirit's guidance on this journey.

Preface

As a child I was always somewhat of a church mouse, going with my mother as she attended her altar guild duties and also being drawn into the worship services at our little Episcopal church with more interest than some of my friends. I loved the beauty of the old Episcopal prayer book and hymnal. I also loved being outside in nature. For a few years I went to elementary school in a different town than where we lived. When the weather was good I loved to walk home through the woods and across a small creek. It seemed so peaceful in those woods and I loved being part of nature. (In more recent times I can't imagine any child being given that same kind of freedom!)

Most summers my family also spent some time at my grandfather's camp on a small lake in the Adirondacks. What could be more perfect than an early morning trip around the lake just as the sun was rising over Old Elephant Mountain? I liked to paddle "Indian style," silently, without taking my paddle out of the water so as not to disturb any of the wild critters in the area (or the boy in the camp on the other side of the lake). Other times, I loved to simply sit in my canoe in the middle of the lake on a windless afternoon. There again I could feel as if I were a part of the mirror-still lake and surrounding mountains. I've learned since that these special times were probably my first awakening to the contemplative side of myself, though I wouldn't have been able to name it then.

Adulthood brought new interests and activities- marriage to my wonderfully supportive husband Len and the birth of our three children. I took a break from full time work for a few years until they were all in school, and then had a variety of jobs none of which could be called a vocation, but they did help to pay the bills. As the children grew I began to ask what I would do if I could do anything I wanted to. The answer always seemed to come back to going to seminary to become an ordained clergywoman. That was reinforced when I decided to try a course to see if I really liked it or if it was my imagination talking. It was a long time since I had been in college so I wasn't sure how the academic scene would fit. Amazing, I did very well. So, another course, and once again I did very well. I loved every minute of those courses. Four years later, with much support from family, friends, my pastor, and church, I was ordained in the Presbyterian Church USA, and almost immediately was installed in my first pastorate, a small church about 45 minutes from home.

Despite my love of the academic world and institutional church, the moments in nature, Biblical meditations, and life in general continued to speak to me of "Something More". Sometimes even the evening news or morning newspaper leads me to notice a theme that runs beneath what is literally before my eyes and ears. For a number of years, I've been drawn to the Celtic Christian notion that God speaks to us in two books, the Bible and Nature (all creation). My spirit is also nurtured and re-energized by times set apart at a spiritual center where I can walk in the fields and woods or just sit in silence. These retreats help me remember and grow deeper in the awareness of who and Whose I am, and how much all creation is connected. And, just pausing by my little stream during a walk in the neighborhood can bring a gift for my spirit.

Over many years, I have kept a journal about some of my experiences of seeing "more than" what was right before me or maybe seeing more deeply. These have come out of daily life- family at home, long walks in the woods, some of our travels, reflections on the evening news, etc. The practice of journaling my reflections is an integral part of my spiritual life, helps me to remain centered and to reflect on the activities of the day or week. It is these journals that I have "mined" when writing this book.

If my words inspire, comfort, or reassure you, if they nudge you to change, or perhaps suggest a new path to follow, I will be grateful. My hope is that within these pages you will find occasional moments of inspiration, and a window that opens onto the sacredness of all life. Happy reading!

Messages from the Stream

I

Spring

Message from the Stream

It's mid-February as I write this and we've got a lot of snow on the ground with temperatures dropping to almost zero each night. My little stream, some call a rill, is totally covered with about 30 inches of snow. I can't see any sign of it below its heavy white blanket. Yet, experience tells me that the water is still there, hidden from sight, running deep below the surface. The message I hear also is that this is the way of the Great Mystery I call a loving God. I have always been able to trust that Presence even when I can't see, feel, or hear it. I am grateful for this reminder.

~

What or whom do you trust to be always there for you?

~

The Morning Sun

I have often been drawn to the beauty of the shadows on the walls cast by the morning sun: beautiful patterns of light and dark, pictures made by lamp shades and window mullions, flower and houseplant arrangements.

In certain seasons like spring, a crystal that hangs in our kitchen window above the sink casts lovely rainbows all over the walls and down the hall. That sunlight also has a way of revealing the dust on the family room table, the spots on a child's picture on the stairway wall, or the dog hairs on the kitchen floor. Oh, how I hate to be reminded of the cleaning that needs to be done!

And then one day I heard the message: that the sun of God's love enlightens all of life—the places within our hearts that need to be cleaned, as well as those that already are quite lovely. Nothing is hidden from the Holy One. Rather, that healing Love can reveal those places within us that we alone often might not see nor want to see, and in that revelation can also begin the process of healing and freeing that which sullies the image of Beauty as originally created.

~

What did this reflection remind you of?

Signs of Spring

The groundhogs have told us to expect 6 more weeks of winter, and they may be right. But, many days when we take our large and elderly lab for his walk in the nearby county park, we follow part of a road that leads to a covered bridge. Recently during a pause between the great snow storms of this winter we noticed the first sign of spring. The snow drops are blooming! It always feels so exciting when we see them, small as they are, only about 4-5 inches high, with little pure white cups hanging from the top, and bright green spikey leaves all around. The cluster of these aptly named and beautiful snow drops seems to grow wider each year, and we love it. Like this year, they often have to poke their heads up through the snow. These fresh, pure white snow drops are for us a sign of hope- hope for the warming days of spring, the arrival of longer days and evening sunsets, and always a reminder to look for signs of hope and new life even in the darkest, hardest, most broken times.

～

Pause and reflect on what are the signs of spring
or of hope in your life?

A Rainy Spring Day

I walked in a warm spring rain today, sheltered by my giant blue and white umbrella. And over and over again in my mind, the refrain of a song sang itself in pace with my footsteps:

> Oh Great Spirit, earth and sky and sea;
>
> You are inside and all around me[1].

A few years ago, in my denomination, after a powerful women's conference in Minneapolis, this was a dangerous song to sing. I didn't understand why then, and to this day I still don't. These lyrics ring out with the chimes of harmony and oneness with all creation.

Even on this rainy day, Creator must smile at the lyrics and pray that indeed all may be One.

∾

How do you respond to the notion of God within and all around?

A Lenten Observance

The traditional observance of Lent has often revolved around fasting from meat or sweets or a bad habit. The idea was to foster penitence, which would lead to a deeper faith and preparation for baptism and or, Easter. However, such practices often became an excuse to lose weight or stop the bad habit. While those might be laudable goals, they too often have little to do with deepening the spiritual life.

Once I saw an alternative observance that seemed to offer an original alternative: taking time for little "Sabbaticals"—brief times out from daily work. Does the car need to be cleaned today? How about the kitchen floor? Why not skip your list to to-do items, or your daily email/ twitter check-in? This was not just any time out, but an opportunity for prayer time. You might even imagine there is a permission slip to fill out, giving yourself permission to skip these usually necessary activities, or others that you name. Maybe it will be only a minute or a few minutes, or even praying at several regular intervals during the day, but how about freeing up some extra time for prayer during this Lent?

∾

How might you change your schedule to allow for more breathing or prayer time during Lent?

What daily activities could you rearrange or drop for this time?

Good Friday

Each year we observe Good Friday, the day when Christians observe the death and burial of Jesus. Once I found myself mentally entering the scene, seeing him on the cross, being taken down and laid in that place of death.

What is the meaning of Jesus' tomb, the place of burial for me, for us?

A place of weeping

abject loneliness

sorrow

total rejection

hopelessness

where all the demons and

forces of darkness

reign

Screaming

deafening

silence

Shunned or mourned by all the world

family

friends

enemies

No life

  no hope

    despair

Nothingness

  no meaning

    nor purpose

Lord have mercy

    Christ have mercy

      Lord have mercy

Then, on the third day

    the tomb is

Empty!

Christ has risen

And given us

  new life

    meaning

      hope

        purpose

~

As you reflect on Jesus' death on the cross, and burial,
what does it mean for you?

How does it make you feel?

Daring to Question

Some days, it's just not easy to accept the plain sense of a Bible story. The story of the healing of the beggar who was lame from birth (Acts 3:11-16) is the one that always sends my questioning mind reeling. This particular day had been one of those hard times when I'd found myself to be the skeptic in the crowd. I wondered:

How could it be, this healing?

What is this "faith through Jesus" that the scripture speaks of?

How can faith heal?

What does it mean to be healed?

What is the "perfect health" that the lame man received?

What is perfect health to any of us?

and

What's the use of all this?

Sometimes the questions tumble, and when they do, I've found it best just to let them come. Only then, when I'm empty and have worn myself out with all the questions, am I open to whatever fresh response might be given.

This kind of questioning is not always encouraged, but I think sometimes the path to deeper understanding leads through the questions.

～

Have you ever been afraid to question something?

What are some of your questions about Scripture or life in general?

On the Death of a Friend— A Lament

O grief, where is the solace?

Calling our mutual friend, hearing her tears,
feeling tears ripple down my own cheeks.

Sorrow and grief mingled with gladness

that our friend's suffering is over

and she is at peace.

It happened so suddenly!

Where is the consolation?

I miss her. It's not fair that one

so full of life

should die so soon.

It's not enough just now to say her spirit lives on in us.

I can't move

on from this place

of raw sadness—

not yet.

Don't hurry me with your platitudes.

Don't speak to me now

of the resurrection

and life everlasting.

Only, please

comfort me,

hold me.

Someday I know the grief won't hurt so much.

But now, I miss my friend.

I miss the time we lost when we were out of touch.

I miss the hope we had of her coming to visit

when she "felt stronger."

None of that can be made better.

All of it just is. It has to become part of the soil of my life.

I know that one day

this wrenching grief

will find its place and become a source

of nurturing

for my spirit. Just not yet.

Who said the rough places would become smooth?

Where is that place of hope?

I want to go there, to ask the questions.

~

When have you felt wracked with grief?

How did you survive that time?

Sacred Presence

Imagine it:

A day at home

all day

to live in

Sacred Presence.

Here.

Now.

Not yesterday

or tomorrow.

An ordinary day

in sacred time and space.

Mist rising from the side

of a tree in the park

warmed by the new sun's rays.

Goldfinch couple

in azaleas by the deck

male's colors so brilliant.

Dogwoods on an old road

    to a covered bridge

        a canopy of pink and white.

Ordinary time.

Sacred time.

One.

~

How do ordinary and sacred times blend as one in your life?

Paradox and Contradiction

I used to wonder how I would ever resolve the seemingly conflicting needs within me that tugged in different directions: the need for stability and change, for solitude and community, for freedom and security, for the work of my heart and of my mind.

For all of us, life holds many such polarities. Esther de Waal's *Living With Contradiction* is one of those books that not only touched me unusually deeply but also helped me realize that sometimes we just have to accept these opposing forces, learning to appreciate what each has to offer and how they enrich our lives. What a relief.

deWaal writes:

> But if paradox speaks to my human condition it is also a vehicle for speaking about: a God who becomes a man, a victor who rides on a donkey in his hour of triumph… a God whose promise is that in losing my life I shall find it.[2]

Of course, discerning what is called for at any given moment might be difficult. Maybe I just need to relax and stop worrying about life's seeming contradictions and learn to make peace with them.

~

How do you live with the contradictions or paradoxes in your life?

The Cross

In *Living With Contradiction*, Esther deWaal also writes about the cross in a way I had never before heard:

> "The wood that went to make the cross was taken from a living tree, but a tree that has been cut, shaped, transformed. The process of cutting, stripping and reshaping is never easy or comfortable; it is protracted and painful. Then the cross itself stands there, its main thrust downwards into the ground, its arms stretching outwards, a balance of two opposing forces, vertical and horizontal held together in dynamic tension. Only so can it be life-giving. In that tension lies a most powerful image for what is at work in my own life. In that transformation I must expect to be shaped, formed and re-formed; nor can I ever hope to escape the tension that lies at the centre and makes possible the holding together of the whole."[3]

This sense of the tree being cut down, and re-shaped, even though it is painful and takes maybe a lifetime, connects with my life. I hadn't ever connected the tension that is maintained between vertical and horizontal arms of the cross with the tensions of opposites that I must sustain in my life. I also love to gaze at trees in all their variations and varieties. Until I read this, however, I had not connected this love with the cross. I will love now, even more, to celebrate all there is to see in life as I gaze at the trees on my daily walk.

~

Pause and reflect on deWaal's word to you in this quotation.

The Death of a Tree

One day I noticed that a lovely old spruce tree behind one of my favorite landscaped homes had died. I wondered when it happened, whether it was disease or perhaps simply old age—it seemed so sudden. Whatever the cause, it was surely a reminder that: *To all life there is a season...dust to dust.*

The landscape of that yard will be different now, but still lovely. Without the tree's shade, what new growth will come? What new possibilities will be opened up?

"Do not cling to me," Jesus said to Mary Magdalene. Within myself, I hear the message: *Let go of things and ideas whose season has passed, whether they are "good" or "bad." Make room for new life in your world.*

~

How has the landscape of your life changed over time?

What do you need to release or let go of?

Bottled Tears

You have…put my tears in your bottle.

—Psalm 56:8

What a lovely image!

What would happen if, instead of "bottling up" my tears and holding them back, I let them be bottled up by the Holy One, along with all the tears of the world?

We're so carefully taught to hold back our tears, and yet science teaches us that the very act of crying is cleansing and healing.

Someone once said that tears are our eyes' way of speaking the words of our hearts. Can you imagine Jesus weeping over Jerusalem or when his dear friend Lazarus died? We don't weep over things and people we don't care about—our tears are the gift of love.

So weep, my love, and be made whole.

$\sim$

What makes you weep? Who "holds" your tears?

Eco-Justice

Near Arcata, in northern California, a wildlife sanctuary has been created from land used in the sewage treatment process.

In the 1960s this land was set aside as part of the nation's first experiment in using the natural landscape in treating sewage. The area is still used for third-stage sewage treatment, located just before the treated water re-enters the tidal waters of the Pacific.

Now a major wildlife and bird sanctuary, Arcata Marsh is a stopover for migrant birds. The air is fresh and the marsh water is clean. Paths, benches, and bird blinds located throughout the marsh invite walking, running, resting, and watching. It is a beautiful setting.

This, for me, is part of what eco-justice means: caring for our planet and its creatures in such a way that we are no longer just overly consuming waste waters but are good stewards of our resources.

∾

What does eco-justice mean to you?

A Thin Space

High on a hill overlooking Humboldt University in Arcata, California, stands a forest that has been allowed to return to its natural ways. In this forest are many old-growth redwood trees, and also many stumps of redwoods and other trees that were cut during the forest's logging days.

Once upon a time, humans thought they could create open farmland out of this forest. They were wrong—the cost was too high. They cut and burned the old growth to make pastures, but the redwoods kept returning.

The sturdy survivor trees that make up today's forest grew back from the old trees' roots, stumps, fallen trunks, and branches. Even now, visitors can see many tall, hollow stumps that are burned black in the middle. From the top of one 15-foot stump grows a Sitka spruce, its roots crawling down the side of the old stump. That Sitka grew from a seed dropped into the old trunk's burned-out core. Another tree looks like a teepee that grew over and around a fallen stump.

Some of these old-growth trees are hundreds, even thousands, of years old—their ancestors might have been around to witness the dinosaurs! Walking in this dark, primeval forest offers the feeling of walking on holy ground. The ancient woodland itself feels like a "thin space"—a place where present, past, and perhaps even future coexist... where one might easily move "beyond the veil" to a time beyond time.

A walk in the majestic quiet of this forest brings with it a feeling of reverence, gratitude and humility, for the opportunity to experience "something more" that defies words.

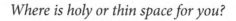

Where is holy or thin space for you?

Memorial Day

My calendar for today tells me to pray for the end of violence. Thomas Merton once spoke of the violence within ourselves that needs attention. I add this to my prayer list.

I begin to think of all the kinds of violence in this world that cry out for healing and peace:

> within and toward myself
>
> within families
>
> within the local and wider church
>
> within our community and nation
>
> among races, sexes, and ages
>
> among those driven by the violence of fundamentalism, like Isis/Isil
>
> against gay, lesbian, bisexual, and transgendered persons
>
> against the differently-abled
>
> against Native Americans, Latinos, and other ethnicities
>
> against those of different beliefs, like Moslems, or Jews
>
> against the earth, sea and sky
>
> against people, places, and creatures I can't begin to name

So much violence.

Help us remember... help us re-member. Help us bring an end to violence and build a new world of peace making.

∾

How would your own prayer list for healing against violence look?

The Knot in the Tree

I love trees in all their various guises… some with branches stretched out to the side like arms, others reaching for the sky.

A couple of trees have caught my special attention.

One grows in the park where my husband and I walk our big yellow Labrador retriever every day. It looks as if someone, some time ago, bent and twisted the sapling's trunk until they created a knot. I've since learned that sometimes children think it is fun to tie a knot in the trunk of a limber young tree. Still, the sapling didn't give up—it grew straight and tall above the knot, and today it is a stately middle-aged tree.

The other tree grows from the side of a rocky outcrop in the Grand Canyon. This tree is old and terribly bent, barely hanging onto life on that ledge. How did it ever manage to grow in such an inhospitable environment?

These two trees are the living embodiment of persistence against adversity.

∽

How or when have you had to persist against an adversity Wilmort, *that would distort your healthy growth into your true self?* which for me has been the place suggested on Page 21.

The New Car

My friend's father wanted to give her a new car. She surely needed it, as her own car's odometer showed 150,000 miles, and the car no longer had air conditioning or reliable brakes. However, she was having a hard time accepting what to her seemed an extravagant gift—she said she felt unworthy.

In fact, this friend often finds it difficult to receive gifts, even though she is one of the most generous people I've ever met. My friend's response got me thinking about how hard it is for some people to receive gifts, especially "extravagant" ones. What about God's extravagant love?

Since much of our faith is lived incarnationally, here is another way of thinking about the car: if my friend rejected her father's gift, was she also rejecting the love of God that came to her through her father? And if so, would she want to do that?

None of us is ever worthy of the extravagant gifts that come our way. That's why we are so overwhelmingly grateful when one is given to us. How do I know this? Because I've sometimes also had to wrestle with my own sense of unworthiness about receiving a gift someone wanted to give me.

~

When have you experienced an extravagant gift, especially of love?

"Stretch out your hand"

One Sabbath day after Jesus had left the synagogue, he met a man with a withered hand.

"Stretch out your hand," Jesus said to the man. As soon as he stretched it out we are told, "… it was restored, as sound as the other" (Matthew 12:9-13). *Bring your pain to me,* Jesus urges us. *Stretch out your hand*—bring yourself openly to me with all that's hurting or injured within you.

Jesus also wants us to help ourselves, too—we must make the effort to reach out to him. Yet reaching out may mean overcoming limiting thoughts and fears: the idea that "I can do it by myself," the fear of reaching out for help. Stretching myself in this way—yielding to his power and love—may be more than you or I are used to doing. In those times I pray:

> O Lord, I come to you. Will you heal my "withered hand"… my withered spirit… my hurting stomach?
>
> O Lord, I come to you, stretching out to reach you.
>
> Will you heal my injured, hurting places, please?

~

What might be your own prayer for healing?

Distractions

Before I sit down each morning for daily silent meditation, I can find an unlimited number of things that need doing.

Before I pray, reflect on the scriptures, and journal, I tell myself, *I'll just do my morning chores.* Of course I must eat breakfast, read the paper, walk the dog, make the bed, and start the laundry. Still other temptations abound. Move the winter sweaters out of the closet. Change the extension cord in my study. Clean the bathroom. Choose the menu for tonight's dinner. And still more: clean off my cluttered desk, put away unnecessary books, then check and respond to emails.

Some of these tasks are reasonable, but not all.

Sometimes my husband will come in and ask if I want to go to the store with him (the answer is almost always yes). Soon the morning is gone!

Oh well, I think, *I can do my meditations in this afternoon or this evening.* But I know that won't happen. Distractions and temptations have won the day.

Time to find another way, I tell myself. So once again, I write out a schedule and prioritize the "must do" activities, separating them from the "can wait" items.

Both the inward and the outward journeys need their time if life is to be balanced. I know this, and still time slips away again and again.

～

*How do you keep a balance of time
with all that calls to you for attention?*

Does this include time for spiritual reflection or prayer?

Examen

An often-recommended spiritual practice is that of *examen*: an examination of consciousness in which we review the past day or other recent period of time, focusing on where we've felt God's love, the activity of God, God's absence, and the like. We ask ourselves questions that may vary somewhat depending on the form of examen. Today, instead of the often-used question "Where have I seen God today?" I asked myself:

> *Where was God's love being shown—manifest—*
> *even if I didn't notice it at the moment?*

Then I asked:

> *Where there was some struggle, difficulty, or strained*
> *relationship, where might God's grace have been in it?*

These small changes made a big difference in my response.

The reframing felt more concrete than the more abstract question, about where was God.

The freedom to frame the questions in an examen to suit your own review of the day can help reveal what otherwise might remain hidden. Doing so, as I did, can give meaning to the activities, events, and conversations of a day by allowing us to "see below" their surface to the meaning within, where the Light is shining.

~

Have you tried an examen of your consciousness about the day in your life?

If not maybe you could try it, being very gentle with yourself.

A Psalm of Praise

Praise to you O Glorious Mystery,
always loving Presence.
You come with Many Names.
I can name but a few.

Praise to you, strong Mother
Who gave and gives me birth,
nurturing me, keeping me safe,
loving me with a constant love,
always present, never leaving.

Praise to you, Washer Woman God.
Forever you scrub and clean the "dirty"
corners of my life, hidden places no one should see,
and lend your inspiration to
my own cleaning chores.

Praise to you, Mother Eagle,
who brought the Hebrews
out of Egypt on your wing.
You fed me when I was young,
nudging me out of the nest when it was time.

Yet still you fly near, and when I am weak
or faltering, you fly beneath me,

that I might rest
on your wing until I am strong enough
to fly again.

Praise to you, Sophia, Lady Wisdom,
with us from the Beginning, always
giving us inner wisdom and understanding—
guiding us like a bright star,
connecting us to the whole earth,
companioning each one as she grows into
her own truth.

Praise to you, Oh Godde,
for all the goodness you bring
            to creation.
By whatever name is given you,

You create and redeem,
support and guide, love
and challenge and encourage us
forever and ever.

Amen.

∿

How would you write a psalm using your own names
for the Mystery we call God?

1   "O Great Spirit", by Robert Gass, Spring Hill, Released this and another song in 1993 on one compact disc.

2   Esther de Waal, *Living With Contradiction: An Introduction to Benedictine Spirituality*, (Harrisburg, PA: Morehouse Publishing, 1997). P24

3   deWaal P15

II
Summer

Message from the Stream

*In this great river of life that flows behind and before me,
let me know that I am carried by you.
In this great river of life that flows around me and through me,
let me know that I carry you
and can reverence you in all that has life.*[1]

One day during a walk by the stream near my home, I became aware that the stream's waters join those of a larger stream just a few fields away. That stream, in turn, joins Mill Creek, which twists and turns until it eventually flows into the Conestoga River and then the Susquehanna River a few miles away. The Susquehanna joins the Chesapeake Bay, which in turn joins the Atlantic Ocean. My knowledge of geography tells me that at some point the waters of the Atlantic also mingle with those of the Pacific—and all are one.

Indeed there is oneness, a unity, about all of creation. We two-legged creatures are part of a much larger whole in which all are individuals, yet interdependent. For example we need oxygen which plants make, and they need hydrogen dioxide which we give off when we exhale. We need each other to survive and be whole.

All is One.

∽

How do you think about the connectedness of all life?

Ordinary Time

Some days are nothing special, and this day was one of those. The world outside was grey and rainy, a warm summer day, and my body ached. Yet my heart felt peaceful, curled up cozily within itself for the moment.

We work and work and keep ourselves so busy that there's not much time "just to be." Yet Joshua Abraham Heschel said, *Just to be is a blessing; just to live is holy.*[2] This quote makes me think sometimes about the violence we do to yourselves by our overwork.

Why do we do this to ourselves? What are we running—or hiding— from?

Maybe the gift of an "ordinary day" with nothing special happening is the gift simply *to be*—to let our bodies and souls heal from the violence we've done to them.

And on the Seventh day, God rested.

~

And you? What is the rhythm of your week or work and rest?

Breathing Lessons

It was to have been a night off for everyone, a breather from the frenetic pace of everyone's life. Our two high school age grandchildren had time off from soccer and baseball practice. Our daughter had an unusual early arrival home and an evening free from church activities. Our son-in-law had an evening free from his soccer coaching. Hurray. This was to be the "once in a blue moon" evening when they were all free to join us for an evening watching the new Lancaster Barnstormers baseball time downtown. This had been a carefully scheduled free evening, but despite the care in planning, activities and events had "mushed in" on everyone anyway, making it hard for some to persist in giving up other activities for this family time together. Frustrations and weariness welled to the surface sometimes threatening to ruin the planned evening at the ballpark. Although we did, eventually, enjoy spending the time together, it took a while as gradually each person settled down and let go of some of the wants and needs and stresses they had brought with them. In later reflection it seems like the evening ended up feeling like "breathing lessons" for everyone. It was a few hours at a slower pace with time to notice the world around us and simply enjoy each other's company. Some would call that sacred time. Perhaps it wasn't planned as such but perhaps that was what was really needed.

~

With each new day comes the gift of time, 24 hours.
How will I use this time? Take time to breathe.

Robot Pool Cleaners

I was away on one of my regular retreats. Because I was away from the usual activities and distractions of life, I was a bit more attuned than usual to the sacred messages sprinkled through my day.

On this particular afternoon, the little robot that cleans the bottom of the pool caught my eye. I chuckled as I watched it calmly going back and forth, back and forth, cleaning its way across the bottom of the pool from one end to the other. Then I wondered:

> *Is this the way you work, O God—*
> *constantly behind the scenes, "cleaning" my heart?*

∾

How is the Holy One at work in your life?

Sunshine and Shadows

While winter walks find me stepping into the sun for warmth, summer walks lead me to seek the shadows for protective relief from the sun's heat. Too much of good thing, whatever it may be, is neither healthy nor helpful. I am thankful that nature provides both sunshine and shadow to balance our various needs.

I'm also reminded of the times when life seems lived in the shadows—those times when God seems hidden, even though my mind says God is still there. Dark nights and shadows come to all our lives, bidden or unbidden, but the Giver of Life is always present. The One who creates will also redeem the hard times, comforting, guiding, and sustaining us on the way.

~

Who provides you with shelter from the heat in the hard times?

Distractions

On my morning walk, there was a truly pesky horsefly that wouldn't leave me alone no matter how many times I batted it away. Distracting to say the least!

Then it occurred to me that this pesky horsefly was like so many things that distract me from what is truly important: the Holy One, and the work I've been called to do. Instead of annoyance, I began to feel gratitude for the insight that I could reframe the "bad" things that can pester me as simply "pesky, distracting horseflies." My prayer is to remember this:

> *"The steadfast love of God never ceases. God's mercies are new every morning..." (Lamentations 3:22-23)*

∾

What word or idea "shimmers" for you in this reflection?

Stay with that for a few moments.

Where Is God?

This is a question that comes to me often. One day the answer seemed, at least for a few minutes, to be clear.

I was in the Philadelphia airport, biding my time during one of a series of delays I'd encountered on my trip back home. It was dinnertime, and I had just set down in the food court with my Chinese food.

One of the low-paid workers was nearby, straightening up the area: sweeping up the bits customers had left behind on the floor, clearing off tables and wiping them down, and pushing the chairs back in. She paused, laying the handle of her broom against the table in front of me. Walking down the aisle through the table area, she returned carrying the tray of an elderly man who had been limping along very slowly. She placed his tray on a table, then hovered nearby while he limped back to the counter to retrieve his travel bag and briefcase and then returned, with equal difficulty. No words passed between them, and as soon as the man was seated at his table, the worker picked up her broom and continued with her work. I couldn't help but tell her what a kind thing she had done for that man.

On that evening, I believe God was in the care and concern of a low- paid food court cleaning woman.

> "Even as you have done it to the least of these, my brothers and sisters, you have done it unto me." *(Matthew 25:40)*

~

Where have you seen love in action or God's activity recently?

Swimming Lessons and Trust

It seems that we are given very big responsibilities in this life to help others float to safety and security through our trustworthiness.

Sometimes we wonder what God is like. This story from an ordinary day about a mother and her toddler daughter gives a clue.

It was a hot, sultry day in August, and an evening dip in the pool seemed like just the thing. As we continued to play, Grace began to trust my hands under her belly to hold her up. Eventually she started putting her hands on my shoulders and kicking her legs behind her, almost like a pro. She even got brave enough to try blowing bubbles two inches under the water.

Supporting Grace as her new skills developed, I found myself reflecting on who has held me up in my life. Whom have I trusted to love and teach me the lessons I am still learning?[3]

Sometimes Godde is like a mom who holds us up—someone so trustworthy that we can risk adventuring into new things. Sometimes God comes to us through a dad or another parental figure who can be counted on to buoy us up in a time of need. I must remember to say thank you to these people, and to God.

~

Who has been there to support you when you needed it?

Jonah and the Whale

The news had just featured a report about a shark that almost swallowed a diver whole. The diver's head and body were all the way inside the shark's mouth when the diver had enough presence of mind to act to save himself. He saved his own life by making the shark uncomfortable enough to cough him back up again. I can almost picture him punching and kicking in that cavernous, toothsome mouth. It was amazing that this man survived with relatively few wounds—thanks not only to his heavy wetsuit but also his own survival instinct and ingenuity.

Sometimes life's trials may leave us feeling as if a whale is swallowing us up and we shall surely die. In the end, though, we are cast up again like Jonah onto the shore to continue our lives. At such times, we may feel as if we've received the gift of new life—and sometimes, literally, we have. It's surely an understatement to say that the diver in the news report was glad to have been "cast up on the shore" of life again.

～

When you have survived a life trial that feels overwhelming, how do you express your gratitude?

July Weeding

Every summer, around July, my little herb garden gets overrun with oregano. That herb seems to want to swallow up everything in its vicinity—the little azalea bush in one corner of the garden, the tarragon, the green onions, and even the lemon mint.

One morning I decided that the time was right for a little pruning, and I took to the oregano with my shears. At the end of my efforts, the herb garden not only looked much better, but thanks to the newly created breathing room, the remaining plants had a better chance of thriving And I came away with a large, fragrant bouquet of oregano flowers to carry indoors for other uses. (Something in me just won't let me throw away any part of a plant that could still serve a good purpose.) In 1 Corinthians 3:6, the apostle Paul says, "I planted, Apollo watered, but God gave the growth." Throughout my morning of pruning stems and pulling the ever-present weeds, this verse had been running through my mind.

To me, this verse reminds us that all we can do is help the plant along: by watering it, giving it good soil to grow in, feeding it regularly, and pruning it as necessary. Ultimately, the growth is up to the plant itself, and the Creator who is its source.

That's not so different from how it is with children, and the church, I think.

~

What in your life could use some pruning or cutting back

to allow for healthier growth of other aspects of your life?

A Little Bit of Heaven

I'm sitting lazily in the back yard in an Adirondack chair, enjoying a long-awaited bit of relaxation. There's a hint of a breeze, with dappled sun and shade from the overhanging tree branches. A baby bird calls out constantly. Ahh, there's the call of the mourning dove—always a reminder of my childhood home in Bethesda, Maryland when it was a far suburb of Washington D.C. The deck's flower pots and hanging baskets are all filled with flowers, and so is the surrounding garden. Before me, the rose garden is in full bloom. Solitude. Beauty. And the presence of the Holy One everywhere around me, in the gifts of this setting.

Praise the Beloved! Praise be to you in earth's sanctuary. (Psalm 150)

Today this setting is my sanctuary, a little bit of heaven, together with my home and family. Who could ask for more?

Let everything that breathes praise the Beloved with their lives.[4]

Yes—with the lives of the trees and flowers, and with all that I am and do, may it be so.

(I want more!)

~

Where for you is a little bit of heaven?

Sunset

There is something very special about sunset. There's a stillness in the air, as if all creation has paused to wait and watch. "Day is done, gone the sun, from the hill, from the sky…" goes the old hymn.

I remember one evening, returning home from my walk with Calvin, our big yellow Labrador retriever.   My husband was relaxing in the rocking chair on the front porch, and we joined him there. The three of us just sat quietly, companionably watching as the colors of the afterglow changed from pink to salmon to red, slowly fading to grey as the darkness of night descended.   As the birds flew toward their nightly roosts in nearby trees, the world settled into the night's rest.

This threshold of night is what some call "the gloaming." For a moment, all the busyness of life slows down, and we are invited "just to be." It's a very pleasant liminal space and time, as the day ends
    and night
            has not
                    quite
                            begun—
        the now
            and
                not

                    yet—

~

Idea: plan to sit outside quietly and simply observe what's happening around you on a summer's evening. What did you notice? How did you feel as you sat there?

The Gulf Oil Spill

As the after effects of the 2010 BP oil spill in the Gulf of Mexico continued months after the incident, I watched in horror as the devastation unfolded. Due to negligence on the part of a big oil company, a connection deep down in the water had broken, spewing millions of gallons of oil out into the gulf. It went on and on, for weeks, and no one seemed to know how to cap it.

What a crime, on so many levels. First of all, against nature—the wetlands and beaches where so many young sea creatures are birthed, the fish in the water and shorebirds, all covered with thick oil. Then, against all the people who make their livings from the Gulf's waters— the shrimpers, restaurant owners, and others in the small seaside communities. And finally, against the large vacation industry—so dependent on the area's beautiful, healthy beaches. Each one, struggling or shutting down because of our collective greed for oil.

The fault is BP's, yes, but blame also rests with those of us whom they supply. We *must* find alternative sources of clean energy.

Creator God, forgive us all—help us repent and turn to a better way to live in harmony with the natural order.

~

*How do you think we could help to be better stewards of this
beautiful planet called earth?
What can you do personally, or what are you doing?*

On the Beach

It was a hot sunny August day at a beach in Delaware. Some friends and I were sitting mostly in the shade of a pergola, watching children playing in the waves. One little boy looked to be totally lost in his own imaginary world, so concentrated was he as he built his sand castle. Oh, that I might always be so present and aware of life, and love each moment of my day!

An ancient prayer came to mind:

> *Be present with us now O Lord.*
>
> *Be here and everywhere adored.*[5]

~

Sink into this old prayer for a few minutes and let it sink into you also.

Love

Love
> holds a child in his arms
> patiently, for minutes on end,
> watching older sisters play
> beyond the frothy tumbling waves.

Then, ever so slowly,
> father and child step
> into the roll of a little wave—
> and still the child is
> securely embraced.

Love's hand reaches
> for a little salty water
> to cool tender young arms.
> A few more steps, and they jump

as one
through a
larger breaking wave.
At long last Love
has carried the child
beyond fear
to the three older sisters.
Love.

~

What picture of love would you create?

Lake Nebo Reflection

Sun's rays shine

    through morning mist on the mountain.

Glory be to You

    for the white rising sun

    and the purity of this moment.

Thump, thump, thump—steady sound of the old green skiff

against the dock when a passing boat's waves

    reach here.

Stillness of early morning.

Light, gentle

    early morning breeze

    caresses me.

Mostly cloudy

    with dappled blue sky

    peeking through.

Gray

    mist creeps up the length of the lake,

    peeking out from around the point.

Peace, be still—
>don't disturb her.
"Old elephant" mountain
>sleeps still
>at the north side of the lake—stability and peace.

I sit on the dock with my morning tea,
>savoring this gift
>of time and beauty.

Thank you, Creator of the universe,
>for this small piece
>of your magnificent work
>and my time at Lake Nebo.

∾

Where do you find peace in nature's beauty?

When Things Go Awry

It had been one more frustrating day in a string of them, trying to complete preparations for leading an upcoming retreat. I vented in an email to our younger son, who is often very wise.

"You have and know all you need within you now," he wrote. His reply fit with the refrain within me that kept saying, "Simplify."

To both Mike and to the refrain within me, I had to answer yes. I knew it meant, in part, that I didn't need all my beloved books to find the answers to my questions. I'd already made this retreat into too much of an effort for both myself and the participants.

Deciding to step aside and let go of the problem for a little while, I cleaned the bathrooms. It felt so good to complete something— to accomplish one concrete goal.

I came away from the household task with some much-needed clarity: although this situation with the retreat had not turned out as I'd planned, perhaps Mike was right—maybe another plan was wanting to happen and my efforts to stick to the original one had been thwarting it.

Once more: Relinquish control, and surrender to the One Who IS. She will guide my steps and, as Julian of Norwich says, "all will be well." Trust.

~

What caught your attention or "shimmered" for you in this reflection?

Strange Languages

In the New Revised Standard Version of the Bible, Psalm 114 describes the Egyptians as a "people of strange speech." What an interesting phrase.

We know the Egyptians and the people of Israel had a poor relationship—it's that way with slavery. But what made the Egyptians a people of strange speech? Did their words sound odd? How did their way of speaking connect to their actions? Was their manner of speech harsh or gentle, or what?

For us today, who are the people of "strange speech"? It makes me ponder the people I've met whose speech sounded strange to my ear, even when we spoke the same language. For instance, I have to listen closely to both South Africans and Scots when they speak, to decipher their words through the accent. This makes me more attentive, which is probably a good thing.

What would happen if we always made an effort to listen more attentively to someone who is speaking—to listen beyond the person's accent or grammar, and hear instead the meaning beneath the words? I wonder if "strange speech" might then invite a new relationship.

❧

Who are people "of strange speech" for you?

How does it affect your relationship with them?

Solitaire

Ever since I was a child, I've always enjoyed playing solitaire. Nowadays I play it on the computer, usually as a mind emptying few minutes of transition from one task to another.

Today it occurred to me that certain aspects of this game reflect principles by which we would do well to live in community: *No card is more important than any other, regardless of its face value.* What matters is the card that's needed at the moment. If the Ace of hearts is out, then only a two of hearts will allow you to build on it. If there is a blank space in the row of cards where a king can go, then you need a king, and only a king will do to fill that space. When the king is there, then the queen can be placed on it, and so on down the line.

Each card has both an individual value and a collective one. Cards have their own unique value in and of themselves. They gain a collective value when they are needed in the larger group.

No single card is a winner. A "win" can occur only when all the cards have been uncovered and placed where they are needed.

"In Christ there is no east or west, no south or north... *All are members of the household and citizens of the realm of God."* [6]

~

What other game might you play that also could be a metaphor

for the realm of God or community of faith?

A Parental Love

Our daughter and son-in-law had a lovely habit when waking their young children each morning. Each of them would hold a child in their arms until the child was awake. What a gift to the children, to have that sense of being loved into wakefulness—a quiet, warm assurance with which to begin each day.

I think that if we are open and attentive to it, this may be how we are all loved into wakefulness in life, by the One who is above and within all of life.

~

Imagine how you would feel if you were being "held into wakefulness".

The Church and Soccer

I once watched my son-in-law coaching a team of preschool soccer players. Mostly he just wanted to get them to stay on the field, away from the sandbox, and go toward the right goal. He spent a lot of time encouraging them, praising them each time they made an effort or actually kicked the ball. He encouraged even their smallest efforts and spoke age-appropriate instructions, such as, "Let's see if we can get the ball into *that* goal with all of us working together." His whole approach was simple, unsophisticated. It also contrasted sharply with that of some of the other coaches, who yelled at the kids for the slightest mistake, seldom praised them, often belittled members of the other team, and shamed their own young team members.

These two coaching styles led me to reflect on what families, and the Church, are about.

On retreat I had experienced, in the deepest depths of my being, that Jesus, the Christ, loves me more than I will ever know—that he wants only good for me, that he will never shame or belittle me or hold my mistakes against me; that whenever I turn to him, rather than holding me unworthy, he will welcome me home, washing and binding my wounds, clothing me anew with garments of faith, feeding me out of his very substance and enjoying my company.

Imagine this as a model for families, or worship, or relationships with others in general. What if, whenever we come to Jesus, we truly were to see him as the Christ—as one who loves us, likes us, and enjoys our company? How would that change the Church, the body of Christ?

Of course the Church would still be imperfect, because we're human—but even so, we would be living out the sacred love of Jesus on earth. We would be showing, through our actions, that imperfect people can come to church to have their wounds washed and bound, to receive nurturance, to be loved simply for being themselves—and those we care for, in turn, would learn how to offer this same healing and nurturance to others, in ever-expanding circles.

~

Allow yourself to imagine some responses to the questions above.

On Reciprocity and Reverence

Have you ever considered how interconnected we humans are with the grass, the trees, and all parts of the natural world? This is true not just for us, but for lions and bluebirds, aardvarks and rabbits, wild salmon and bullfrogs too.

Like most living things, we humans and other animals need oxygen to survive. Daily we breathe it in without a thought of where it comes from—unless we have breathing difficulties because of physical challenges, or oxygen is scarce in our surroundings—and breathe out carbon dioxide. In contrast, the green, growing things such as grass and flowers, bushes and trees, need just as urgently to take in carbon dioxide—and they, in turn, give off oxygen. This is a perfect example of reciprocity: mutual, life-giving assistance.

What a system! It gives me a sense of reverence and awe for the created order, part of the original blessing. It also makes me ponder how we humans might best preserve and restore our environment—if for no other reason than that our grandchildren will be able to breathe when we are gone.

∾

How did this reading connect with its title for you?

A Monastery for Daily Living

Sometimes I need to withdraw from the tasks of daily life for a time and re-center myself. It's not that I want to become a nun—they, too, have a lot of daily obligations. That's just part of living in a community, whether a monastic order, a family, or a commune. Still, there is great value in occasionally stepping aside from the busy pace of life. For me, entering my study can have the same effect as stepping into a monastery for retreat and prayer. I've arranged parts of the room intentionally to create sacred space—with a candle (or flower in summer), perhaps a special picture, or a figurine of a woman with up-raised arms, or something else. These simple items can have a profound effect, helping me quiet down within and return to my center. Someone once said that there is a monastery inside our hearts, a sacred place we carry with us wherever we go, and to which we always have access. I need this sacred space often. How about you?

~

Do you have a monastery at home, or inside your heart?

If not, what would it look like to create one?

The Spiritual Life

For years I've pondered what the spiritual life is, and how to express that in my own words. Many have written about it extensively, but sometimes I need to find my own truth. Here is some of it:

The spiritual life

is like a spirited horse

galloping through the fields

for the sheer joy of it

unbound by conventions

with all its muscles and sinew

stretching, reaching out to meet

the rushing wind

coursing over its neck past its ears and flanks

with tail outstretched, waving gaily

faster, faster

until it stops

and listens

its ears perked up high

turned in that moment

toward LIFE

and its own true self.

The spiritual life

is also like a flitting butterfly

that dances from flower to flower

lighting for long periods in stillness

almost in suspended animation

entering fully, in those moments, into *life*.

The spiritual life is like the horse and the butterfly,

full of life,

and much, much more.

∾

"What are the words for your spiritual life, your truth?"

Sunrise

Some days the sunrise is awe-inspiring. On this particular morning, the sky appeared cloudy until I looked east. Where the sky was slowly brightening, pink edges outlined the receding gray clouds. From a central point rose a column of light that radiated a barely perceptible glow. It reminded me of the light saber's beam from the movie Star Wars.

Suddenly the first crescent of sun appeared below the column, and the single beam widened and split into many lesser beams. Then the sun grew full and blinding—I could no longer look at it directly, only at its effects on the surrounding clouds, sky, and earth. The presence of the light changed everything, illuminating even the darkest reaches of sky. The unfolding beauty was almost impossible to capture in words.

The daily movement of the sun across the sky brings warmth to some places and shadow to others, constantly changing the landscape from dawn to darkness, ever renewing it with each new day. Even on the darkest and stormiest of days, when we can neither see nor feel it, still the sun is there. So it is with Sacred Presence—sometimes hidden from our immediate experience, yet always there to warm and provide what is needed.

∾

How might you describe the experience of Sacred Presence?

Endnotes

1. John Philip Newell, *Sounds of the Eternal : A Celtic Psalter* (Material Media: San Antonio), 65. (part of the Prayer of Thanks)

2. Abraham Joshua Heschel-a familiar quote found in many sources, especially on small banners; here from the Ministry of the Arts, Congregation of St. Joseph (LaGrange Park, Ill)

3. —*The Lantern*, Summer 2009. The United Church of Christ in North Hampton, NH. Used by permission of the author, Michele Bagby Allan.

4. *Psalms for Praying*, by Nan Merrill (Continuum, NY, NY, 2003). The quotes are her interpretations of psalm 150.

5. Exact source unknown; possibly a variation on a table blessing, "Be present at our table Lord..."

6. Covenant Network, PCUSA, Conference theme song

III
Autumn

Message from the Stream

In late summer the water in my little stream runs very low. By the time autumn arrives, the stream looks as if it will soon dry up completely. Rain is sorely needed.

And God's absence? Is this also the way with God? It seems that my little stream leads me over and over to this same question.

I pray:

> Sometimes are You under the surface, running deep? Is that when You seem to be absent? And what "rain" can bring back my awareness of your sacred presence?

~

How, if ever, have you experienced the absence of God?
What awakened you to God's presence even if hidden?

An Autumn Prayer

Canada geese honking
      through their training flights
Crisp sunny morning's
      refreshing air
Orion sparkling in the clear night sky
Spruce tree's fallen twig
      reaches up with outstretched arms—
            embracing arms of the Christ?
Acorns abundant
            some caps still joined
            some single, alone
      one cracked
            What is it within
      that needs to be cracked open,
            set free to grow?
For all of this and more—
      hidden things I have not seen—

Thank you.

~

What do you notice as you walk through autumn?

What inside you needs to be cracked open, and released? Why?

Fog

> *The fog comes in*
>
> *on little cat feet.*[1]
>
> —Carl Sandburg

Recently I'd been reading about autumn fog, and then one morning, there it was—deeply blanketing the landscape with fleecy softness.

Fog invites me to an interior time, to travel through the mists of Avalon to the "other side," to live, even briefly, in that sacred space where "all's right with the world."

Slow down, fog says. *See, hear, be.*

The fog creeps in to remind and encourage us. And the earth gives a sigh of relief.

> Grey mist outside
>
> invites interior silence.
>
> I hear you whisper:
>
> "Come into the cave of your heart
>
> And sit awhile with me."

~

How does fog affect you?

When do you feel the need for quiet, interior time?

Music

It was a time when I felt drained and dispirited by all that needed my attention. My husband and I already had tickets to an evening concert at the concert hall in Lima, Ohio. Though I didn't feel much like going, we went anyway.

The guest artist was Lazlo Fengo, a young cellist. I played the cello myself for many years until raising children preempted the practice time. Fengo's ability to draw rich tones from his instrument was like manna from heaven that revived my soul. What a gift.

How often we forget the healing power of music, art, and drama. I remember reading about how, for the mystic, Hildegard of Bingen, "music re-creates the original harmony that existed between God and [humans]. For [Hildegard], each human heart was a resonant and receptive instrument from which God could draw beautiful tones as from a lyre."[2]

Hildegard also believed that hell was the place of no music! (I believe her!)

That evening, listening to Lazlo Fengo draw beautiful music from his cello, I felt a sense of that original harmony—a little bit of heaven.

~

How are you affected by music, or particular instruments?

Do any instruments bring you particular peace and a sense of harmony in this world?

"Matter Matters"

Lord George MacLeod, founder of the Iona Community in Scotland, was known to say:

Matter matters because at the heart of the physical is the spiritual.[3]

Today more than ever, many people are concerned about the future welfare of planet Earth. It is now critical for earth's survival that we rethink our stewardship of earth's resources, and that we pay attention to how all life—plants, animals, birds, fish, and humans—are interrelated.

When a small snail from the Far East is carried into the Great Lakes, where it has no natural predators, it can multiply at unimaginable speeds, clogging drainage pipes and doing endless harm. Yet how often do we think of the physical matter of earth including our own bodies as being something that affects our spirituality?

Matter matters. We have been created as one small link in the great chain of interlocking pieces that make up all of creation. Every creature has its purpose, its place in the matrix. We humans have been given the special responsibility to attend to the welfare of this planet.

Have you ever thought about how you might be praising our loving Creator when you recycle a soup can rather than throwing it away? Or when you make the choice for or against a certain financial investment? How does making healthy choices for your own body praise the Creator?

Screensavers and Attention

Contemplative living involves learning to be attentive to what is being experienced right in the present moment—"staying in the now." But what does this phrase actually mean?

Recently my computer screensaver gave me a clear sense of the answer. I've gathered many of my favorite photos from various times in my life into an electronic file folder called "Interesting Pictures," for my screensaver to use as a scrolling slideshow. The folder includes snapshots from a trip to Scotland and Iona, a granddaughter's soccer game and prom, visits with cousins, flowers from Longwood gardens, a snow scene from a favorite retreat center, and many others.

These pictures flash across my computer screen for only a few seconds. If I want to see them, I must slow down and give my undivided attention to each—right now, no distractions allowed—or, poof, the image is gone.

What a joy it is to simply sit and watch these wonderful memories pass before my eyes one by one. Gazing at a picture of a brilliantly colored autumn tree, I often will see something I never noticed before and appreciate the gift even more.

Ironically, these screensaver pictures of times past have reminded me how important it is to be deeply attentive to what is happening in the present, in each moment along the way.

～

Stop. What is before you or in you right now that wants to be noticed?

Good for Earth Day 69

Two Books

A favorite hymn for many people today is "For the Beauty of the Earth" which reflects a sense of awe at the divine mystery interwoven throughout the natural world. The psalmist also speaks often of the natural world, praising God:

> *The heavens are telling the glory of God;*
> *And the firmament proclaims God's handiwork. (Psalm 19:1)*

> *Praise the Lord…Mountains and all hills*
> *fruit trees and all cedars!*
> *Wild things and all cattle*
> *creeping things and flying birds* (Psalm 148: 7, 9-10)

Many of us were raised on the notion that God speaks only through the Bible and the Church. How freeing it is to discover that the Celtic Christians deeply loved the natural world and saw it as an expression of God's glory.

The ninth century Irish teacher, John Scotus Eriugena, spoke of the two books of God's revelation: the Bible, and the natural world. Indeed, many of the high standing crosses in Scotland have Biblical scenes carved on one side and scenes from the natural world carved on the other.

This brings to mind a walk I took when I saw a little brown squirrel sitting on a nearby rock, staring at me. I wondered what it might have been saying. Could it have been a word from Creator?

~

How does the natural world speak to you of divine love?

Words

Most days I spend a little time reflecting on the lectionary—the day's appointed Biblical readings. Sometimes it's the story or lesson that becomes my focus, and sometimes it's the words and phrases themselves. When I read the words slowly and carefully enough to hear them deeply, they are so descriptive—for instance, Psalm 114:4: *The mountains skipped like rams, and the hills like young sheep.*

What a beautiful landscape these words evoke. Imagine how being too literal would ruin it. Poetry, whatever its source, is not meant to be taken literally.

Secular words, and The Word—how closely related they can be, when we use words as they are meant to be used: with gentleness and precision, to say what we mean, and to mean what we say.

～

Where have you caught yourself being too literal
and missed the poetic or metaphorical meaning of something?
Ask a friend, or the Holy One
what meaning they see in the passage.

God's Will

How often we hear people speak of God's will. *It was God's will that he should recover from his illness,* or that *she should go to Dartmouth College,* or that *he was not meant to be on the plane that went down.*

How could a good God will bad things such as the Holocaust, or 9/11? I always wondered what kind of God would select good things for some but not for others. It just didn't make sense.

So what is God's will?

Maybe it's that God wills good for all people, even when bad things happen. This makes sense to me, along with the idea that God stands with people through bad times and good—suffering as we suffer, rejoicing as we rejoice.

I once read that the Greek word for will means "yearning." *God yearns for the wellbeing of all God's creatures and creation.* Yes.

Thinking of God's will this way makes sense of Isaiah's words:

When you pass through the waters, I will be with you.... (Isaiah 43:2)

～

Imagine God walking or sitting with you in love
during your own dark, hurting time.
What does that feel like?

On Losing My Place

I was about four months into my ordained ministry. Everything had been going so well. I had it made! Or so I thought.

Then one Sunday while leading worship, I made three mistakes that had to be covered or corrected before the end of the service. I forgot to include the "Minute for Missions" in its intended place and so slipped it in after the introit. I totally lost the second lesson, discovering I had marked the wrong one—and then I couldn't find the right one. And then during communion, I forgot to serve the bread to two elders. O my goodness! All I wanted was a deep hole to crawl into.

But I made it through the service, and the lunch with two "important" parishioners afterward, even though by that time I had no appetite.

Afterward, as always, the congregation was very forgiving. About the lesson, some even said they liked the way I told the story when I couldn't find the right place in the Bible, because it seemed more real to them. Yet, no matter how forgiving they were of my errors, I couldn't forgive myself. I wanted to run away—from the church, and more, from myself.

Before the day's end though, a gentle ripple of love from friends and family enfolded me. They let me vent my frustration without trying to fix anything, and they all affirmed me in turn as pastor, friend, mother, or wife. I became more aware than ever of how much we need others, a whole community of family and friends, to help us through the difficult moments: to hear us, to care for us, and to love us, however we are in the moment. My own struggle also helped me become sensitive to some who I knew were struggling with loneliness or unworthiness.

Surely this is the work of Spirit, blowing through our lives.

∾

How does my story touch your own truth?

Peeling Apples

Peeling apples,
>   making mincemeat.
Healing my soul—
>   contentment.
Autumn sun
>   dancing on my cutting board.

Len puttering in the garage:
>   rhythm of nailing
>   brackets to the wall
>   hanging bikes old and new.
Sounds of a baseball game
>   coming from the garage.

The rhythm of life:
>   Wash, peel, chop, measure.
>   Wash, peel, chop, measure.
>   Mix, cook, can.

The sun sets gently
>   behind the trees.

Autumn.
>   Peace.

~

Reread this reflection a few times, including once out loud.
What image stays with you? Why?
Carry it with you through the day

Watching the Moon

Evening:

    sitting on the rocking chair

        in the little alcove

            my sacred space.

Before me, past the window

        a stunningly beautiful

           white saucer moon.

I watch awhile as it dances

    with the tree's top branches

        before it sets.

Then I close my eyes

    in silent prayer.

When I open my eyes

    my beautiful moon is gone!

Sadness

    until I look more closely:

        the moon has only moved

in its orbit

    above my window now

        and out of sight.

All I need do is

    change my position

        and all is clear again.

Joy!

Changing my perspective:

    is that all I need to do

        to find You again?

hidden things I have not known

Gratitude!

            ~

When has changing your perspective made a positive difference?

Walking the Labyrinth

As I walked the labyrinth on retreat
a soft voice asked:
What do you see?

> Harvest fields
> Miniature webs on the boxwood
>> like little white Christmas decorations
> Red leaf
> Flowers scattered here and there on the path

What do you feel?

> Cold on the rock in the center where I sat to pray
> Warmth from walking
> Cool air on my cheek
> Pain in my hip at times

What do you hear?

> Traffic passing on the nearby road
> A symphony of birdsong
> Your voice within my heart saying
>> *Trust me*

What do you taste?

> Red raspberries from nearby bushes

For everything that is—

> thank you, Dear One.

～

*What do you see, hear, feel, or taste that brings a word
of thanksgiving to your heart?*

Evening Prayer

The day is over now.

"Day is done; gone the sun," says the old hymn.

What has been done

is done.

What has not been done

is not done.

A blessed day.

I leave the day and the night in your hands, O Holy One,

and will rest in your loving arms this night.

〜

How does this reflection connect with you, or not?

Computer Hard Drives

My computer's hard drive is meant to be always working in the background—to keep on whirring away no matter what, tracking all the programs I've installed to do my work. I trust it to do its job behind the scenes, and usually it does. When it crashes, though, the results can be mind-boggling.

The one whom I call God is a bit like my computer's hard drive, but reliable! It's comforting to know She is always there, operating in the background in love—One who persistently and lovingly creates, redeems, and heals; whose spirit will always be there to comfort and guide me through life.

Unlike my computer's hard drive, God is never subject to power outages, worms, and viruses. It's phenomenal to realize that working behind the scenes in my life is One who is always present—not only for me but for the whole world, all the time.

∽

How does this resonate with your image of the Holy One?

Think of another image that works for you?

Love, and Sacred Love

How do you define the word *love*? It's so real and life-giving, yet so hard to capture in mere words. Yet sometimes I still try. I experience sacred Love and love in the beauty of…

Each day's new sunrise

A blooming cyclamen

A misty, interior day

My spouse's gentle touch

Our son's welcome phone call

A church member's greeting

Our puppy's wet licking kiss

The peace of this moment

And a thousand other goodnesses.

Love is in all that is good and beautiful!

～

What does love mean to you?

Roadblocks

Some days it feels as if there are roadblocks everywhere I turn.

At work I had made my supervisor very angry, although I couldn't understand why. It wasn't the first time our interests had collided, and each time it happened it came as a surprise. I felt mystified and trapped, angry and sad. Tears of frustration and fear were close to the surface. I could see no good way to turn, and roadblocks on every path. Unless we could reach a new understanding, I could see no other way out except to leave, and that would also mean abandoning some wonderful people. As has been true for me so often, the daily scripture readings gave me hope during this anxious time.

First:

> *Let your speech be always gracious, seasoned with salt*
> *so that you may know how you ought to answer to everyone.*
> *(Thessalonians 4:6)*

I take the word *salt* to mean God's steadfast love, which invites me to remember it is always present, and to do as well as I can.

Second: Jesus's words to the woman with the alabaster jar became his words to me:

> *Your sins are forgiven. Your faith has saved you; go in peace.*
> *(Luke 7:3ff)*

These words encouraged me to persevere with renewed strength and prevail during this hard time. At a presbytery meeting, colleagues' words of support seemed especially graced, warming my heart. Others also added their words of encouragement. I knew I was not alone.

Soon a psalm continued this encouragement with words of Wisdom:

You have proved us just as silver is tried...
[and] brought us back to a place of refreshment.
(Psalm 66:10,11)

I do not believe that God deliberately sets difficult tests or roadblocks in our path. I do believe that when they come, as they will, we have the opportunity to grow stronger in faith and love.

At last, after some time and hard work, my supervisor and I reached reconciliation. Along the way, I had gained insight and inspiration, and that was enough.

~

How do you approach difficult situations?

Is it effective or does it need to be changed?

Tuning Forks

When I played the cello and needed to tune it, I would strike the tuning fork, hold the end of it against my cello, and listen for the note to which I needed to adjust the strings.

The tuning fork reminds me of the standards, values, and beliefs to which we attune ourselves when discerning how to respond to questions and challenges. These principles can give us a true note with which to tune our discernment and decisions.

Thinking of this reminds me to ask myself what my tuning fork is telling me today.

~

What is your inner "tuning fork" telling you today?

Little Sayings

Retreat centers often have little sayings posted here and there on the walls, sometimes with author's name, and sometimes not. Once while I was on retreat, I found one that read:

Behold God

Beholding you

And smiling.

"You are precious in my eyes

because I love you."[6]

To me, these quotations are like little parachutes of grace.

～

What little quotations feeds your spirit?

Satisfying Our Hunger Within

As I am writing, our country is in a deepening recession born of greed and heaven knows what else. Perhaps many today would profit from a prophet's word.

The book of Haggai in the Hebrew Scriptures begins with a description of all the things with which people have tried to fill the empty spaces within their hearts, and the effectiveness of those efforts. The prophet arrives on the scene asking if this is the time for them to live *in paneled houses* while the house of God *lies in ruins*. The prophet asks how well they have fared with all their sumptuous living and acquisitiveness.

Then he says,

> *You have sown much and harvested little;*
> *you eat, but you never have enough;*
> *you drink, but you never have your fill;*
> *you clothe yourselves, but no one is warm;*
> *and you earn wages but put them into a bag with holes.*
> *(Haggai 1:6)*

The next section speaks of the consequences of such wastefulness, but perhaps the recession that has overtaken our country spells that out clearly enough for now. Finally, the prophet challenges the people to rebuild the temple, to place their hearts and minds and actions in a place that is pleasing to God. He is inviting the people to a totally different way of life—one that is much richer and more abundant than the one they have been living.

Some people today are still trying hard to fill the God-shaped hole within their hearts with things: mega-mansions, giant TVs, the latest automobiles, clothes from Prada, and other luxuries. And yet how rich we can become when our hearts are filled with that holy Presence we call God. Of course, we need a minimum of food, shelter, and other essentials for healthy living. That's not what the prophet is speaking about; it's the **excesses**.

For those who depend on material acquisitions to satisfy the insatiable hunger within, it can be scary to give up their "stuff" and turn to that which will truly feed their spirits. But God reassures us, toward the end of the passage from Haggai: *I am with you, says the Lord.* (all the way, I add.)It seems to me this passage is not only about acquisitions and excess but also **attitude**. What is the **focus** of our lives—the **center**? We might ask how each person, place, thing, and activity of our day might show us something of the mystery of God. This is what's important.

This passage cautions us not to mistake the symbol for the substance of our real focus.

∼

How true does this reflection ring in your life?

"A Mutual Balm for the Soul"

How often do we stop to consider the truth in the scripture that says, *As we give ourselves in love, so we receive love?* The author Nan Merrill speaks of this mutuality in her version of Psalm 147:

> *The Beloved abides in our heart,*
> *in every open heart that welcomes Love.*
> *Through Love we are sent to the brokenhearted,*
> *a mutual balm to the soul.*[7]

When my mother knew that someone was feeling down, she often wrote the person a letter. Even if she was going through a hard time in her own life, her practice was always to write only about the good things that were happening. In so doing, she would lift her own spirit.

I wonder—was it for the mutuality of care that mother was always tending to others? Is it this sense of mutuality that makes me feel better when I do so, too? This mutuality of need and benefit seems to be God-given, built into our DNA.

"Give and you shall receive," says scripture, and so it is, it seems, with a mutual balm for the soul.

～

What does mutuality in love mean to you? Think of an example.

Silence

We are told God's language is silence, yet how often do we not even allow even a few moments in the day for true silence. It's been said that music is really all about the rests or spaces between the notes. They bring order and beauty to the piece. Without them, the notes would sound like boring chaos.

I wonder how I might monitor my own speech so that it includes periodic rests—silences that would allow me to listen more carefully, attentively, and fully to the speaker in front of me, whether the speaker be another person or God?

◁◦▷

Idea: Notice how your own speech patterns
include "rests between notes".

A Psalm for the Grand Canyon

God you spin the whirling planets,
and through the eons have created
the beauty of our natural world.

River water flows deep
  in the wide canyon now
and the winds wear away
  the rocks above.
Layer upon layer of strata revealed:
  table rock, red rock, white rock
  layer after layer
  down to the bottom far below
  where still the water flows on.

You are creating still,
deep within this canyon, and in
  the depths of my soul…
    below the surface
  desert trimmed with
    green shrubs and trees.

Looking out from above
across the vast reaches of this great and grand canyon
I see indescribable, wild
untamed beauty.

"In the beginning"
    wildness
        wilderness
and Holy Spirit moved over all
    creating
        carving
            shaping…
Living water ran ever deeper
    always untamed
        creating
        carving
            shaping…

So big, beyond imagining
You are—
    so big,
    beyond being tamed
    or brought under control,
    mine or anyone's.
    Yet still, like the wind and water,
    always shaping, creating,
    forming and reforming.
Praise to You, O Creator
of the universe,
the Grand Canyon, and
my life.

∼

*Try writing your own psalm about a place
that has filled you with awe and wonder.*

The Spiritual Guide

My spiritual guide walks with me on this journey,

helping me to notice the life around me on the path

and make connections between me and that life—

as with the strands of the spider's web—

there is pattern

    sacred and holy.

~

Who walks with you on your own spiritual journey?

Red Rocks and Snow Drops (All is One)

Red rock canyon, snow drops and crocuses
Hale-Bopp's fuzzy brightness
Moon's slow eclipse
Quiet dawn and azure river
Laughter on the phone
Quiet evening with partner and friend
Sorrow as one slips away
Joy as another returns
Uncertainty of employment
      or living location.

The mourning dove's call and robin's early song
      greet this day,
      singing me to wakeful
      attention.

Loneliness—and solitude
Anger, rage—and peace, serenity
Fear—and confidence
Loosing—binding
Freedom—and constraint
Wholeness surrounds the fragments,
      drawing order from chaos.

Peace—Shalom—Integration
Wholeness of all life
All is one
God

          ~

How did you connect with this poem?

Waiting at the Grocery Store

My husband and I had been out grocery shopping and doing a few errands together. We had forgotten one item at the grocery store. It seemed silly for us both to go in, and since I had not brought my purse with me, I waited in the car for him to return. As I sat quietly, I began to truly see what was in front of me and nearby—to experience my seeing in a different way. I didn't have paper and pencil with me at the time, but I reflected on my experience after we got home.

Waiting, I see:

Landscaping around the new bank across the street.
A woman carefully watering the mums just outside the store
    (that's why they look so good, I think).

An SUV parking in front of our van with a mother and young daughter,
    the daughter dancing delightfully on a nearby curb.

It's a cool, sunny autumn day
with bushes arranged carefully
by one corner of the store,
their leaves varied: smooth and sharp, red and green and deep gold—
never noticed them before.

Beauty so often goes unnoticed.
I see around me a world
alive with energy
a symphony of sounds
a weaving of colors and activities.

But first I must pause,

and sit…

and wait…

before I notice

what is right there—

before me.

~

Suggestion: try writing your own poem
about some very ordinary experience?

Where does it lead you spiritually?

Endnotes

1   Sandburg, Carl *"Fog"*. This poem has been frequently anthologized. Perhaps the earliest was *Untermeyer, Louis, ed. (1919), Modern American Poetry, Harcourt, Brace and Howe.*

2   *Hildegard of Bingen: and Her Vision of the Feminine,* by Nancy Fierro (Sheed and Ward, pub. 1994) p23

3   As quoted in *The Book of Creation: An Introduction to Celtic Spirituality* by John Philip Newell (Paulist Press, NY 1999), p5

4   *Sounds of the Eternal: Meditative Chants and Prayers* by J. Philip Newell, #2 Chant: Hidden Things

5   *Sounds of the Eternal*

6   Source unknown

7   *Psalms for Praying* by Nan Merrill, (Continuum, NY 2003) p305f

IV

Winter

Message from the Stream

Winter invites some different ways of doing things than other seasons.

It was warmer than some days and the sun was warm on my face. As I walked I felt the invitation to follow a different path. I also walked a bit farther than I usually do, though I still paused for a moment at my little stream.

Just this little shift in routine made me feel lighter and lifted my spirits. It's amazing how such a small change can make such a big difference.

Some people seem to be satisfied with following the same path all the time, while others need variety to feel alive. I wonder what drives this need for novelty—is it curiosity, a fear of sameness, the joy of new experiences, or something else?

How does a small shift in your normal routine affect you?
How does winter cause some shifts in your routine?

Drowning

When our children were young, I would take them to the nearby college pool for Monday evening family swims. Once, as I stood nearby talking with another woman friend, I suddenly became aware that my youngest child was simply *sitting* on the bottom of the pool. Although he was in the shallow end, the water was well over his head. Yet he looked quite contented. Immediately I was in the pool, reaching down to pull him up to air and safety.

Another time, while I was away on retreat, I had another experience of my own during a period of deep meditation: like my young son, I felt as if I were drowning, and it was not bad at all. I felt calm and contented. Yet suddenly, in my meditative state, there were hands reaching down to pull me back up again to life.

Both times led me to a sense of joy and inner peace—one from being savior, one from being saved.

How closely related these feelings are, though they come from very different perspectives.

∽

Who needs now to have someone reach down into the depths
of their drowning and pull them up to safety?
Is it you, or someone else? How does it feel?

John the Baptist

One Advent, the pastor of the church we attended put a new spin on John the Baptist. His question still resonates: Who is John the Baptist for you? Who, for you, points the way to Christ?

Who? I asked myself. My mother, my childhood pastor, my first spiritual director, a few people in churches along the way, and, many others.

Often it was not so much what these people said but how they lived and loved. They did not preach at me about the "shoulds" and "oughts" of life—instead they showed me a genuine concern and care born out of their own relationship with the Christ.

At my home church, both the pastors and the people were fully engaged in a nonjudgmental, welcoming ministry that emphasized balancing the service of worship with their service in the world.

Each Advent I still pause and ask myself, *Who is John the Baptist for me today?*

～

Who is John the Baptist for you?
Reflect on that experience for a few moments.

Train Whistles

Once upon a time my family and I lived in a mid-west community where six train tracks crisscrossed the landscape. It seemed as if trains ran all day and night, though of course they didn't. Most people became so accustomed to them that they no longer heard the whistles—they had become part of the normal background noise. But we were new to that community, and I heard them.

For me these train whistles became a little gift of grace. Each time I heard one, no matter where I was or what I was doing, I would pause for a moment of prayer. It might be only a brief word, *God*, or maybe a phrase, *for this day/meeting/person, thank you*. It wasn't possible to interrupt every activity I was engaged in, or people would have thought I was crazy. These were interior prayers anyway, and no one else needed to know about them.

Since then we've moved to a different community, but I still look for something that will be my "train whistle."

~

What calls you to prayer, or to pause for a moment of awareness and attentiveness to that "something more" in life?

Hildegard of Bingen

The twelfth century Benedictine nun Hildegard of Bingen is one of my favorite mystics. Among her many gifts was a special language she created. One of her words, *veriditas*, has to do with the greening of life. When we are feeling shriveled up and dry, we lack veriditas. When all is well, we are filled with veriditas, and life has a sense of moistness and fullness. It's much the same as with the trees in the woods near our house. The ones that are dying are obviously dry with brittle branches, while the living ones are pliable, with green leaves and moist interiors.

For Hildegard, the lines between metaphor and reality blur. If all our being is alive, then every time we encounter the color green, we encounter the aliveness of God—we are a part of God's greenness. Still, not all things are the color of green, but show their aliveness in a fullness and fruitfulness of their being. Mary, the mother of Jesus showed her fruitfulness—her greening power—in giving birth to her first son, a part of the incarnation.

~

Ask yourself as I do sometimes, how green, how alive, am I today?
Where might I find greening power, fruitfulness?
Where is the living water to quench my thirst?

Epiphany—Twelfth Night

(Twelve days after Christmas)

For the gift of this day,

> gratitude.

And for the number twelve.

> Twelve tribes of Israel.

> Twelve apostles.

> Twelve months in the year.

Our grandson is twelve.

Twelve hearts on the card.

Twelfth Night,

 Epiphany, and the light shines

> with a startling brightness

> that brings such incite and wisdom

> as wants to be shared with all world

Twelve.

Oh, the sacredness of this number

⁓

What other number is sacred to you?

Where does light shine in your life? Who or what brings it?

Valentine's Day

Love is an irresistible desire to be irresistibly desired.[1]

—Robert Frost

What a delight to be able to surprise my love with a gift of roses. He has given me so much over the years, and not just materially—most of all his love, demonstrated in so many ways. His choice of a Valentine card is always just perfect. I marvel at how he chooses just the right cards for everyone and every occasion. It's a part of the thoughtful, giving person I love. It's true that there is great joy in giving, maybe even more than in receiving. And although a person is not God, on Valentine's Day, I am reminded of how Love becomes incarnate in special ways in my life partner.

∼

How have you experiences Love incarnate through another person?

An Evening's Reflection
Based on Psalm 103:1

Bless the Lord, O my soul,

  And all that is within me,

  Bless God's holy name.

   Bless the Lord, O my soul

    In the evening

     And in the morning,

  Washing the laundry

    Or the dishes

    Or my body.

   Bless the Lord,

    Driving to work

    Or in my morning walk.

   Bless the Lord,

    As I sit with one who grieves

    And phone the one rejoicing over a new baby.

   Bless the Lord,

    On sunny days

And rainy days

And muggy or blizzardy days.

Bless the Lord

With my aching back

And dancing thoughts.

Bless the Lord

In sickness and in health

Poor times and better

Employed or unemployed.

Bless the Lord

At all times.

Bless the Lord, O my soul,

And all that is within me,

Bless God's holy name.

~

How did you feel about this psalm reflection?

For what might you want to "bless the Lord?

Welcoming the Stranger

Our lovable black-and-white cat, Hobbes, was 15 years old and had been our only pet for two years when our 33 pound yellow Labrador puppy Calvin arrived. There was no welcome mat from Hobbes! Rather, with arched back and much hissing, he showed how bent out of shape he was at this unwelcome intrusion into his kingdom.

After the initial hissing, Hobbes withdrew to other parts of the house and presented a very "stiff body" to us whenever we tried to pick him up. Very disapproving! We encouraged him, spending time upstairs with him, putting his food where he could reach it easily without going into the kitchen.

Gradually he began to accept, if not like, this intruder. Sometimes it seemed as if he was taunting the little guy—no friendliness at all. He was determined to assert that this was his space, and he wanted the intruding bundle of canine energy to be very clear about that. Once Calvin, already twice Hobbes's size and still growing, became submissive before him, things got better.

So much for welcoming the stranger in our midst, as scriptures tell us to do. Gracious hospitality takes hard work, whether we desire to offer it or the need to do so is foisted on us. Our cat reminded us of that, very firmly—although after a few months together, Calvin and Hobbes could be seen curling up together.

∾

Who is "the stranger" in your life?
How hard is it for you to be welcoming?

What do you do to try to be more welcoming?

Life's Lessons

Bringing our adorable but large puppy into our lives when he was just three months old reawakened my husband and me to the early years of parenting: the new puppy woke us at night, required frequent and immediate attention, and needed constant vigilance from us to keep him (and our living room) safe from harm. He wanted to taste or eat <u>anything</u> that came near his mouth!

Calvin came to us after our three children were grown and long gone from home. The difference between our lives with a puppy and our lives "back then" with three human babies and toddlers was parental perspective and maturity. Both of these are hard-won gifts, born of years of living. There's no other way to receive them. I am grateful for all those years of living with the joys and sorrows of being a parent, and the struggles and wisdom that came with them.

~

What gives you perspective and maturity?
What gifts have you have received in life?

Psalm 147

Hallelujah! How good it is to sing praises to our God! The Lord rebuilds...

gathers... heals... binds up... counts stars... calls by name...

is wisdom beyond limit...lifts up the lowly...

—Psalm 147 selected parts of verses

There are so many ways to describe the activity of God. How can we know God?

I think one way is simply to look around—to notice the goodness of creation, the healing of relationships, the liberation of people from both internal and external "prisons," and the making of justice. Where I see promise, hope, support, and encouragement, compassion, mercy, etc. from and for others, I think *there*, is God.

Nan Merrill's version of Psalm 147 also reminds me of the mutual benefits of shared love. *For as we give ourselves in love, so we receive love. Through Love we are sent to the brokenhearted, a mutual balm for the soul.*[2] This mutuality of need and benefit seems built into the cosmos, maybe even God given.

~

Where in the world today do you see
all the activities of God that Psalm 147 lists?
God help us to see, truly see, today.

Ash Wednesday

On this day some religious traditions observe a rite of ashes: placing a smudge or making a cross of ashes on the forehead or hand of each worshipper. Traditionally, this has served as a reminder that we all came from the same stuff and will all return there one day—dust to dust, ashes to ashes. They are also reminders of both our imperfect humanity and our mortality. But there is another way we might think of these ashes: as stardust.

I've heard it said that we all come from stardust—that all humanity is created from the same elements. NASA's spaceship Stardust brought back actual samples of the original stardust that began our sacred community of life on planet earth. How can we not respond first with a sense of awe and reverence? And then of humility?

Ashes to ashes, dust to dust—all are one in a sacred community that includes all creatures, all flora and fauna, of the earth.

∾

This Lent, what difference might it make if we "sprinkled stardust" all around us each day?

And, what do we need to surrender in our current life in order to even be aware of the "stardust" within ourselves, and become more one in the community of all earthly creatures who share these common elements?

Six Things God Hates

How recently have you stopped to consider, not what God loves, but what God hates?

It's not something I do often, but a reading from Proverbs 6:16-19 brings me up short. It tells me the Lord hates:

> "haughty eyes, a lying tongue, hands that shed innocent blood, a heart that devises wicked plans, feet that hurry to run to evil, a lying witness who testifies falsely, one who sows discord in a family."

What a list! These are things for me to remember—to ponder in my heart, and to put next to all the good things God loves.

~

Which of these caught your attention?

Stay with that for a few minutes, and ask what it is inviting you to.

Are there others that you might add to the author's list?

Name some of the things God loves.

Idolatry

Proverbs 7:1-7 was the lectionary's reading for the day. In the particular Bible I was using, this subsection was titled "False Attractions of Adultery." However, upon reflection, I thought the passage spoke of something beyond the literal adultery we hear about so often on the evening news, as when one senator or another strays from his marriage. Verses 4 and 5 give a hint of this:

> Say to wisdom, "You are my sister," and call insight
> your intimate friend, that they may keep you from the
> loose woman, and from the adulteress with her smooth
> words.

The kind of adultery the Proverbs passage refers to seems to be about the seductiveness of thoughts, things, and activities that lure us away from true faithfulness to our first love—the love of God. All of these interesting and seductive opportunities seem to be a temptation to idolatry. Putting anything or anyone before our first Love, the love of God, is very close to the adultery this passage speaks of.

In Matthew 11 Jesus tells his disciples, "take my yoke upon you." What if this first Love is the "yoke" of which Jesus speaks? How easy it would be to bear a yoke that "gives rest." The modern world's temptations, whether in the form of material things or relationships, feel like mere idols compared to such an invitation.

～

What thoughts, things, and activities lure you away
from your first Love which is God?

Rainy Days and Sunshine

"Bask in some sunshine," my wall calendar suggested. But today was yet another cloudy, rainy day in a week of such days. I could tell myself that the fields and trees, tomatoes and zinnias needed rain, but enough is enough. I needed a break in the cloudy, rainy days. I wanted some sunshine!

So I had to go within, into my heart. And there, after a while, I did notice all the goodness and sunshine around me, both in my home and in this world.

~

God of the universe, God without and within, guide me this day.
Let me not be grumpy and wear a frown this day, but be attentive to
where the sun is shining, even metaphorically.

Bring Many Names

Bring Many Names, beautiful and good, celebrate,
in parable and story, holiness in glory, living, loving God.[3]

"Bring Many Names" is a song about all the names for God. One day as I made my daily devotions, I started listing all the names for God in the Bible: Holy One of Israel, Creating Spirit, Weaver, Strong Warrior, Yahweh, Father, Mother, Potter, Love, etc. There were so many!

But how do you name a mystery? How can you bind up love and box it in with a name? It's disturbing, even approaching idolatrous, when only one name is used to the exclusion of others. The beautiful hymn quoted above helps me to celebrate some of the breadth and depth of this One we call the "living, loving God".

~

How many names for God come to your mind?

Passing Over the Crack

It was a lovely week for some serious reading at Chautauqua, New York, and I was staying in the Presbyterian house. Meals were served family style, with identical dishes of meat and vegetables placed at either end of the long table, which actually was two long tables that had been placed together end to end, as one. Newcomers quickly learned that one did not pass food "over the crack" where the two came together—that is, until one night when the single dessert tray had to be passed down the table's whole length!

Change.

When our mealtime pattern changed, it caused consternation among a few people and amusement among others.

~

What might we learn from our reactions
to this one simple disturbance of the normal routine?

Dawn

Before me

    the horizon is sharply etched

    all below is darkness

    all above bright with yellows and reds.

Gradually the landscape

    lightens

    as above the horizon

    the dawn grows brighter,

    shining the new day's light

    over all.

Oh, may the dark landscapes of my life

    receive the dawn of faith,

    and hope, and joy

    and love,

that shine from the Light above

until all is one in the Living Light

                 ~

One day, why not pause and watch the sun rise
and its light dawn upon the earth?

Spacious Places —
A Constriction of the Heart

In a tense situation, when fear or anger constricts my heart, I often ask God to help me pray the psalmist's prayer—to remember that, although times are hard, "yet you have brought us to a spacious place" (Psalm 66:12)

A spacious place—what a lovely phrase! It feels so much better than the tightness I feel within. My head tries to tell me I can handle anything, and that whatever it is, it's not that bad anyway. My gut too often yells otherwise. Perhaps the constriction I feel is just my little-girl fear of daddy's wrath, showing up again.

Whatever it is, I pray:

> *Dear God, let tension and fear be gone, and may my heart*
> *and my attitude be open, spacious, and hospitable toward you,*
> *and all I meet, including—or maybe especially—*
> *those I would call enemy.*

~

What is your prayer when stress and tension and fear reign within you?

Spacious Places — A Stirring of the Pot

Sometimes what I call "a stirring of the pot" occurs in the life of a family, church, or community—a time when things get all stirred up by someone's attitude, prejudice, or actions, and the hurt that had settled to "the bottom of the pot" muddies the water once again. This time the stirring happened because of a hurtful letter one family member sent to another, although I don't suppose the sender intended it to be so. (Intent doesn't always make any difference, does it?)

When such a stirring happens, where is the hope? Psalm 66:11-12 says it well:

> *You let people ride over our heads;*
>
> *We went through fire and through water;*
>
> *Yet you have brought us out to a spacious place.*

When anger wells up in muddied waters, may I always look for the spacious place in my heart where steadfast love, justice, and mercy live, and hold to steadfast purpose born of these three.

~

How does this prayer fit your desire for a spacious place within?

A Mystic's Wisdom

At times when life's challenges and confrontations seem overwhelming, the wise words of the mystic Julian of Norwich are worth recalling.

> And these words, "You will not be overcome," were said very insistently and strongly [by Jesus], for certainty and strength against every tribulation which may come. He did not say: You will not be assailed, you will not be belaboured, you will not be disquieted, but he said: You will not be overcome. [4]

~

What is your response to Julian's words?

The Spiritual Life

The Spiritual Life

    feels the fire and the ice of life

        feels the anguish and pain

        of deep hurt and sorrow

        feels the lightness of glee and joy

        of grace-filled moments

            happiness—the heights of joy

            whirling freedom—feels connected
            by zillions of filaments

      to trees and stars

      to friends and family

      to all life as part of the Divine,

          the sacred, the holy

          to all

          as part of Mystery

             beyond words.

The spiritual life

　　says *come* to life

　　eat *this* bread

　　drink *this* cup

　　invites me to be fully alive

　　　　and present to my life *now*

　　　　enfolded in and informed by the past

　　　　anticipating the future

　　　　but living *now.*

Come, feed on me, feed on life,

　　NOW—fully alive

　　with thanksgiving.

∽

How does this reflection connect
with your own understanding of the spiritual life?

"*Of course*"

Our son Mike and I were talking one day about how to express the inexpressible. The gospel for that Sunday had been about Jesus's transfiguration on a mountaintop. When three of his disciples were mystified by what they saw and experienced, words eluded them. Some people speak of "Something More" when they refer to the mystery of what others call God.

A way Mike had found to speak the inexpressible was to use the phrase "of course." For him, those words spoke of exquisite moments when we have entered, ever so briefly, into sacred Mystery. They conveyed a sense of being on the path—in the perfect way of nature's truth.

Even today, words still elude us when we try to speak of sacred Mystery. Perhaps "of course" is one among many ways to speak of this illusive Mystery. It seems to affirm the manner in which all things are created as part of a whole, a oneness. Of course!

~

How do you find words for the inexpressible mystery beyond knowing?

Hospitality

When I began visiting various Benedictine spiritual centers for retreat, I was touched by the amazingly gracious hospitality and consideration with which I was treated. At that time it came as a pleasant surprise, but now I know that hospitality is part of the Benedictine path.

Often I would arrive to find a welcoming small vase of fresh flowers on the dresser in my simply furnished and always clean room. On one visit the sister who greeted me learned that I like a cup of coffee in the morning, and from then on, fresh coffee was always waiting for me when I emerged from my room in the morning. My every need was attended to. Sometimes I even felt as if a protective bubble surrounded me so that I would not be disturbed.

Perhaps most striking for me was the honoring of silence. This was silence of a different kind than I was used to, one that spoke of a caring community. When I would occasionally pass a sister in the hall, she would offer a silent, friendly greeting with a little nod of her head. If I needed something or had a question, I could leave a note, and later I would find a written response under my door. No unnecessary speech was allowed to interrupt these days of prayer and meditation.

Since then, I've wondered how much of a typical day is filled with idle chatter.

~

What does hospitality mean to you?

How can respectful silence be part of hospitality?

A Healing Story

...do not fear, for I am with you, do not be afraid,
for I am your God. I will strengthen you, I will help you,
I will uphold you with my victorious right hand.
(Isaiah 41:10)

For many years I've followed a lectionary in my denomination's *Book of Common Worship Daily Prayer Book*. More than once, its rich Biblical readings have healed my wounds, sustained me, given me strength, and helped me celebrate life. I never know what to expect when I begin to meditate on them, and occasionally they seem dry.

On this particular occasion, I'd been going through one of those tough times that come along in life. I was almost at the end of my rope—in fact, I couldn't even "tie a knot" anymore. Tears were close to the surface, and I wasn't sure how much longer I could continue the struggle.

The appointed reading for that day was from the Hebrew Scriptures, Isaiah 41—the words in the short quotation above. The words of that passage were living water for my parched spirit.

As I sat with them on the page before me, I felt my broken spirit being made whole again. And I knew that with the help of the Holy One, I would indeed be able to survive this troubled time.

This mystery always amazes me—the gift of grace.

~

How do the Isaiah's words from the scripture above feel for you?

Endnotes

1   *8 of the Best Quotes on Love from Poets Who Might Surprise You*, by Leah Sutton. "Love is an irresistible…" Frost was quoted as saying [this] in a 1957 review of *A Swinger of Birches* by Sydney Cox. Now a very popular saying found in a number of places.

2   *Psalms for Praying: An Invitation to Wholeness*, by Nan Merrill (Continuum 2003), P306f

3   *Glory to God: The Presbyterian Hymnal* , Westminster John Knox Press (Louisville KY, 2013) #760

4   *The Wisdom of Julian of Norwich*, compiled by Monica Furlong (William B. Eerdmans Publishing Company, Grand Rapids, MI 1996) p18

CPSIA information can be obtained
at www.ICGtesting.com
Printed in the USA
BVOW03s0815160417
481386BV00001B/145/P